76 *for Philadelphia*

Also by the Author
TO REASON WHY (Poetry)
THE ITALIAN-AMERICAN NOVEL (Criticism)
PRIMO VINO (Poetry)

76
for
Philadelphia

To Andrew Hook,
With respect,

Rose Basile Green

Rose Basile Green

April 2, 1976

New York: A.S. Barnes and Co., Inc.

London: Thomas Yoseloff Ltd

© 1975 by A. S. Barnes & Co., Inc.

A. S. Barnes & Co., Inc.
Cranbury, N. J. 08512

Thomas Yoseloff Ltd
108 New Bond Street
London W1Y 0QX England

Library of Congress Catalogue Card Number: 75-34771
ISBN: 0-498-1862-8

ACKNOWLEDGEMENT

The works of art illustrating the poems are reproduced by courtesy of The Pennsylvania Academy of the Fine Arts (pages 17, 21, 27, 30, 34, 37, 58, 64, 73, 84, 96) and The Historical Society of Pennsylvania (pages 25, 39, 43, 53, 55, 57, 62, 66, 68, 101, 103), and the Author gratefully acknowledges their cooperation.

Printed in the United States of America

CONTENTS

5

TO PENNSYLVANIA

This Pennsylvania, score of everything!
From ions scaled where stars belong,
It cues the spheres, making the whole world sing
Iambics of the human dream in song.
It squares its forms like dactylls dyked in rhyme,
Containing well-springs where all lyrics flow;
The rows, like verses, measure growth in time
To harvest epics from the lines we sow.
Its cities are anthologies of art,
Translating granaries to streets and walls;
The universities remap the chart,
Unlocking carrels to reprise in malls.

Her voices pitch parades in tune to freedom's mime,
That string to band the bell to ring the word sublime.

TO PHILADELPHIA

I care enough for Philadelphia
To sing my faith in her, and to exhort
Her vantage point. The woods above are clear,
Though to the South she is a major port.
Her arms hug mountains, stretch to pet the sea,
Embracing farmlands, suburbs, and near towns;
By clasping park and university,
Her heart with every culture beat abounds.
Museums, music, talents, and the arts
Are jewels that her wedded finger bares,
The legacies the founders left, those hearts
Who pledged her covenant in open squares.

A citadel to house fraternity,
Penn's Town is green with love's eternity.

INTRODUCTION

For two hundred years, the continual framing of the concepts of human freedom, recorded by the indelible signature of the architects of our national precepts, has forced the visitor to Philadelphia to make a rendevous with history. This slim volume of poems is an attempt to extol this meeting-place, the metropolis which has preserved the Colonial town where the American nation was born.

The reader is invited to make a tour of the city whose innumerable notable places demonstrate the reason for calling it "every American's native city." The returning American will also find here a community that is totally contemporary and vigorously alive with educational, cultural, scientific, and recreational institutions and facilities. Philadelphia to-day **is** the Bicentennial City, a great modern seaport, the industrial Workshop of the World, a center of business and finance, a mecca of the arts, a city of homes and educational institutions, and the scene of effective social developments.

In these poems, I confess to the inevitable commitment to this city that any visitor might make who adopts Philadelphia by choice. To come to this metropolis is to become part of it. But especially important, I believe, is the tenacious effort expended by the city's volunteer women working in every area of civic activity. For this reason, I wish to commend **The Women For The Bicentennial** who share in the projection of this volume.

These lines are offered as an effort to assist all Americans and admirers of American to laud Philadelphia and its participants in the Bicentennial. To celebrate is to **THINK '76.**

RBG

WHY PHILADELPHIA

I hear the city singing in the streets;
I see the rainbow highlighting her face
As she treads lightly, prophesying sweets
For everyone who dares the market place.
Hers is the prerogative of love,
Seducing enemies of touch and grace;
As once she smiled from structured steps above
The stranger, pilgrim floundering for brace.
The day she spied his pockets stuffed with bread,
She spiced the air with laughter of her wine;
Then, in his home, she bowed her courtly head,
And now their quiet elegance is mine.

This city, cradle of eternal youth,
Is rocked by parent freedoms, arms of truth.

INVITATION TO PHILADELPHIA

This sphere of earth upon its axis turns,
Fed by the vapors of eternal fog;
Its source, the fire of the sun, still burns
To mark in time the scriptures of its log.
There was a second split upon this globe,
That heaped the splinters on a mingling pile;
A nation formed and grew, that others probe
What seedlings gave it form and forged its style.
They ploughed its back and mined it to the heart
To find the rootings spreading from a mall;
In this city, where others had their start,
They chart their groves from Independence Hall.

This Philadelphia, this port of green,
Invites the world to all that it has been.

A BUS RIDE

From Barren Hill to where the streets are trees,
The wheels trail through Andorra on the way
That wanders like a pilgrim when he sees
The wonders now about to charge his day.
Watch eager Roxborough brick up its house
With grades that buttress banks of falling streets;
Each duplex shading partridges and grouse
Until the cobbled road the river meets.
The secret-bosomed Schuylkill slithers on,
Uncoiling murkily the boat-house rope
To spill the cherry blossoms from Nippon
And give the slought-off Eucalyptus hope.

As Septa bridges over City Line,
Penn stretches out his arms and he is mine.

THE SKYLINE

The skyline is a fugue of blinking themes,
Reflecting rhythms of the rising sun;
As I approach it from my broken dreams,
I am assured of all that has begun.
The star-struck hives of industry are cued
To prop the stage to orchestrate our toil;
The squared tops have with City Hall renewed
The pact that William Penn would have in foil.
The rising boxscape notes our enterprise
Recycling into symphony the beat of Mars;
The twilight revs the river bank of eyes,
Stage overheads that dim the light of stars.

The tune the world transposes at its best
Is phoenixed in this pitch-blende of the West.

WILLIAM PENN'S CITY

On City Hall is towered William Penn
Who came to claim his Woods in eighty-one;
He quaked old prison walls for New World men
And planned the province for a city's run.
He gave to Philadelphia her name,
The city with the love new brothers give;
Then for the Declaration primed the same
Revved theme that makes the Constitution live.
Spread eagle of the law, gave freedom wings;
Nor war nor bloodshed marred his boundaries;
His asking message of the Kings of Kings
Won us the wampum belt for centuries.

He showed that peace pares talons in the end,
And turns the stranger to a sharing friend.

PENN'S TREATY WITH THE INDIANS

When Penn signed treaties underneath the trees,
The elm of Shackamaxon topped his pact;
Among the men were bent no wounded knees;
The open branches armed their every act.
One of the West paid homage to the truce,
Who with his brush immortalized the vow;
As art in nature mitigates abuse,
The artist's work reveres the spirit now.
The purple hues that shade the chieftain's mark
Blend well below the greens that lift with hope;
They gird the tree, a stone in Treaty Park,
That points the method for our way to cope.

Confronting masses battle with the body's force,
While bargained peace pens back the mind to every source.

PENN'S TREATY WITH THE INDIANS
Painting by Bejamin West

BICENTENNIAL CITY

This is the city of America,
The point that drew the letter of the dream;
Now is the time for us to honor her
And rub the starshine of her pristine gleam.
This was the focal spot where we first made
Resistance as a record of our pride;
In sixty-five, the Royal Charlotte stayed
Unloaded of the stamps we all decried.
Like silence that deflates the lion's roar,
Indifference will wear all fury out;
The one small stand will lead to many more;
The forking whisper zooms into a shout.

The first refusal to submit to tax by stamp
Was the blueprint for protest that peopled every camp.

PHILADELPHIA TEA PARTY

The word came in September, seventy-three,
To make our townsmen at the State House say
That levied tea was on its way by sea
Without consent of citizens to pay.
Eight resolutions fused to light the cause
In mid-October's hallowed time to flare
Within three weeks to burn the Boston laws
And choke the Harbor with the party ware.
On Christmas Day, a Polly dressed, arrived
To sail the Delaware the pilots matched;
They led her Captain Ayres by ways contrived,
And back to England had them both dispatched.

The Tea Party to dare our freedom's thirst,
Like other things, our town has had the first.

CARPENTERS' HALL

In seventy-four, the port of Boston closed,
The people looked to Philadelphia
To call a Congress where the lead was posed,
Corraling strength from stormed hysteria.
Once more Revere the warning message rode
That flanked to spur the delegates to race;
The Hall the carpenters had built and showed
Gave for their running time its virgin space.
In Independence Park, still hitched it stands,
Its harness and its traces daily groomed;
The masters kept its manege for their hands,
While Pemberton and New Hall service roomed.

The Georgian face its regal brick retains
That stalls the craftsmen bridled for their gains.

JOSEPH PEMBERTON
Painting by James Claypoole, Jr.

THE FIRST CONTINENTAL CONGRESS

The meet was made of men who marked and showed
They might a Plan of Union rights explore;
The Adams, doubled, George and Patrick towed
To rally Congress, late in seventy-four.
With Randolph of Virginia, President,
They bowed before Duche in their first prayer;
As Secretary Thomson penned, they bent
Controls into Association there;
John Dickinson their Declaration wrote
Of Rights and Grievances they put to list;
They pledged for British trade no more to float,
And use of foreign goods they would resist.

The Continental Congress was the norm,
The first that gave democracy our form.

CHARLES THOMSON, SECRETARY

Short-lived authors dim to light the great;
They hold the pen and note the winds of storm,
As our Charles Thomson, not a delegate,
Helped the Assembly the First Congress form.
Schoolmaster, tradesman, Continental scribe,
His signature the Declaration shows
The hand of service cannot all describe
What is immortal with the ink that flows.
But history makes dear the artifact,
The home that dubbed Bryn Mawr on the Main Line;
Laid out by William Penn as one "Welsh Tract,"
Our Schuylkill can old "Harriton" define.

Men of action, straining after fame,
Depend on writers who would use their name.

THE RESOLUTION

A swelling in the land, by seventy-six,
Kept growing with the Paine of Common Sense;
The delegates from states made brews to mix,
To vote the cosmic war-head—Independence.
On June, the seventh, Richard Henry Lee
A resolution from Virginia gave,
That the United Colonies be free
As States, with rights to be and none enslave.
Then, a committee formed, no time to lose,
A written Declaration to prepare;
The great prescription that the world would use
To cure the people's cancer of despair.

Decision is the trigger of the act
That blasts the lightning dreams to thundered fact.

CONGRESS VOTING INDEPENDENCE
Painting by Edward Savage

THE SECOND CONTINENTAL CONGRESS

The tenth of May, in seventeen seventy-five,
The Congress met in our State House to sit;
For they had stood to watch the fighting drive
That Lexington and Concord shot with grit.
They formed the Continental Army, charged
To George, our gentleman and general,
Who went to Massachusetts and enlarged
The Navy and Marine, now federal.
The sea spawned heroes for the Commodore,
First Ezek Hopkins, then our John Barry,
Lieutenant John Paul Jones, who dared with more,
Followed by Nicholas at Tun made starry.

Like minds must meet to measure out the might
To make ideals come real with arms to fight.

THOMAS JEFFERSON
Painting by Asher B. Durand (after Gilbert Stuart)

THE DECLARATION OF INDEPENDENCE

The Declaration is the artifact
Of human dreams that, fed with freedom, grow;
It is the polled event, the project pact
That terms the document for law to know.
The words that Mazzei phrased for Jefferson
Improved our Franklin, and John Adams, too;
Then, Thomas with his pen, his only gun,
In the Graff House wrote out what they would do.
The Congress met on that July, the fourth,
The resolution to adopt in print;
John Nixon read it to the crowd come forth,
Upon the eighth, to hear our written mint.

This was the parchment of the first degree
We doctored for the nation to be free.

THE MEN BEHIND THE DECLARATION

The train of independence rode on wheels
That grooved on tracks laid down by freedom's sons;
We hear their sound unspoken in the Peale's,
The ringing words that engineered the guns.
Charles Thomson, modest secretary, stares;
While Richard Henry Lee in profile leads
To phrases Thomas Jefferson still shares
Of lines Mazzei taught him from older creeds.
John Hancock of the Congress, largest hand,
Displayed, as president, that large-script force
. More than an art-drawn face his name would brand,
A signature above SFB Morse.

Independence National Historical Park
Enrolls in art the heroes and their mark.

GEORGE WASHINGTON AT PRINCETON 1779
Painting by Charles Wilson Peale

WASHINGTON CROSSING

When, battered in New York, they sought retreat,
Across New Jersey into Pennsylvania,
They watched the British sweeping south to seat
A victory in Philadelphia.
That frozen Christmas night in seventy-six,
Our George with his two dozen hundred men
Recrossed the river's broken ice to fix
The Hessians in the Trenton-Princeton pen.
These battles won, our city was intact,
Like sage Minerva with her crown unspoiled,
Reserving for the heroes myth and fact
Inscribed in mounds on banks where they had toiled.

Rebirthing buried spirit bogged in flight's despair,
Renewal crossed out failure on the Delaware.

THE BRITISH TAKE PHILADELPHIA

Once failed, in seventy-seven Howe sailed back
From Chesapeake to march from south by land
To where our George tried the advance to crack,
But broke at Brandywine upon the strand.
On that eleventh day, September wept;
Defeat now nursed the wounded Lafayette;
At autumn's prime, by night, the British crept
To massacre Wayne's men, Paoli's net.
Then, on the twenty-sixth the victors camped
Where now the Hill Society is known;
By Lancaster to York our Congress ramped;
Our bell we floored to hide in Allentown.

There was a music stilled of every beat,
The sound that waits the silence of retreat.

THE BATTLE OF GERMANTOWN (OCTOBER 4, 1777)

At Stenton, the James Logan Mansion housed
Commander Howe, whose three-mile line was drawn;
Troops through the heart of Germantown were roused
To meet our George at Worcester at dawn.
The General his men marched fourteen miles,
Four roads the columns in the night to prong;
But at the dawn the fog confused the files;
Each fought the other, seeing nothing wrong.
The victor at the Chew House, Cliveden, wrought
The treachery that reamed the gifted horse;
As Washington before Billmeyer sought
The truce, the carrier was struck by force.

While the usurpers storied the defeat,
Our Trojans for a new world took retreat.

STATE HOUSE ON THE DAY OF THE BATTLE OF GERMANTOWN
Painting by Peter Frederick Rothermel

THE BATTLE OF FORT MIFFLIN

In Philadelphia the British stood
While Washington cut their supplies by land;
Their food was low; for heat they had no wood;
The iron-pointed timbers stayed their hand.
Above those dangling dangers frowned defense,
Fort Mercer in New Jersey, Mifflin here;
The dragon of their hunger forked offense
With land and naval forces, front and rear.
On that November tenth, by day and night,
They bombarded Fort Mifflin to the ground;
Two-hundred fifty men in death took flight;
The others scorched the earth and left the sound.

As the retreat rallies in his camp,
The victor drinks his wine, and burns his lamp.

DAWESFIELD

In the valley of the Marshes he remained,
Once the General from Germantown reversed;
He started on the legend that he gained
As a stage sleeper in a play rehearsed.
For twelve days at October's end he stayed
At Dawesfield, home the Morris built and own,
Rejoicing there to hear Burgoyne was flayed,
Surrendering at Saratoga town.
While Franklin made alliance with old France,
Our George held courts-martial in living gown,
Removed Paoli's shame, made Wayne enhance,
Withdrew upstairs, while Lafayette limped down.

Like brave Aeneas trapped in the designs of Jove,
Our Washington was master of both the sword and glove.

GOUVERNEUR AND ROBERT MORRIS
Painting by Charles Wilson Peale

PHILADELPHIA TORIES

The Tories, local Borgias heaped with gold,
Had faith entwined with vine leaves of the crown;
The Shippen to the André title sold
To stage the Meschianza in the town.
In May of seventy-eight the ball was blind
To know in June the British all would leave,
When Arnold, Governor, would stay behind
With Peggy, that his fortune might conceive.
He planned with André all West Point to give
To royal forces by conspiracy;
Discovered, went to England then to live
And left his treachery as legacy.

The empty house, Mount Pleasant, is a testament
That treason bears its home no arms of government.

VALLEY FORGE
Watercolor by H. Faber

TO VALLEY FORGE

On misty days I hear the fifes and drums
Above the whining wind along Ridge Pike;
The hallowed music with the traffic hums
Where Nature Center scouters take their hike.
Beneath the tar old imprints of gone feet
Bleed holes into the corpuscles of ground;
And where the bandage spilled their wounded heat
The meadow of the Forge is now their mound.
Beyond, where Lafayette embanked the hill,
The roads roll up and down in fantasy;
There, wheels seek sanctuaries for freedom still,
Where continentals mustered ecstasy.

At night, the stars cross gold upon the snow;
Free spirit must within a valley grow.

THE HEADQUARTERS

In storms they strapped their bows at Valley Forge,
The hero setting camp with Isaac Potts;
One day the ironmaster saw our George
Upon his knees in prayer behind the lots.
Deep in a thicket, with his God alone,
He shrank beside the sapling to one side,
The growing tree flanking the house of stone
With its new strength the master's horse kept tied.
Here, still, behind the picket fence, the wind
In rattlings of the shutters time rotates;
The news of the Alliance turns the mind
That George with faith and muskets celebrates.

As ferric cutters smithed the General to stay,
Another iron hewer so forged our name today.

END OF THE WAR (OCTOBER 19, 1781)

Firm Philadelphia resurged once more
As war-time capital in seventy-eight;
New articles at the State House, the core,
To sign Confederation came the eight.
The Mazzei Plan to win had Washington
With Rochambeau at Yorktown set the trap;
They caught Cornwallis, and the war was won;
A rider bore the word, a two-day gap.
Aide Tilghman brought the folded, bulled dispatch
For which our Congress in Thanksgiving prayed;
Then, on our city streets where all could watch,
The captured flags, full twenty-four, displayed.

The Church Reformed reveres those men today,
Where there and at St. Mary's you may pray.

SURRENDER OF CORNWALLIS
From a French Engraving

THE UNKNOWN SOLDIER OF THE REVOLUTION

To dub the patriots who for others died,
In Washington, the Square, there is a tomb;
There neither sunlight nor the dark can hide
The stone memorial that roofs their home.
There, once, the British had the city jail,
Then, as a military prison used;
The wounded, too, were littered there to bail
The dying who in common graves were fused.
Time has no count for those without a name,
Who fell when protest purged the foreign crown;
They breached to show the perfidy, the shame,
Of serving nations other than one's own.

The country has no more a fitting place
To lift a monument, their common face.

THE CONSTITUTIONAL CONVENTION

A wester in the storm stirs elements
To crystallize the freedom on the wind;
Convention in the spring breeds governments
To fuse the trackless blowing of the mind.
Twelve states gave fifty-five to sound the air,
From May the twenty-fifth six days a week;
But chemistry in silence fixed their fare;
No one about the work would ever speak.
Led on by Washington, the President,
September seventeenth, they all approved
The final form of Wilson's draft, and bent
To hear sage Franklin who for union moved.

This distillation of legality
Was our first chart of unanimity.

ADOPTION OF THE CONVENTION

We, the people, never end debate
Between consent and signing on the line,
As, in the absence of no single state,
The document bore names of thirty-nine.
The quick to ratify was Delaware
To lead the states to June the twenty-first;
By April, eighty-nine, thirteen were there
To launch the nation with a global burst.
At the Historical Society
Lies the first thesis of our argument
That to each ghetto gives priority
To list its brief and voice its sentiment.

The Preamble of all our discontents
Still works to mend and level off our dents.

CAPITAL OF THE UNITED STATES (1790-1800)

In 1790 the first Congress met
Like beavers digging marshes by the trees;
At Sixth and Chestnut for ten years they set
Their logs to mark the course for unknown seas.
The house there semi-circled the first floor;
The Senate scurried to the room above,
Inaugurating Washington once more,
Presiding with addresses that still move.
The paths they tread through thickets horned and dark
They cleared to words the Advertiser made
Which now the Inquirer hauls back to mark
The speeches that no dams of silt can fade.

The President is first, as Henry Lee said then,
In war, in peace, and in the hearts of countrymen.

HOUSE OF DECISION

Lord Sterling quartered on the Delaware,
Housed by the Thompson-Neely families;
There Washington, in council, plans laid bare
To cross the river from the guiding trees.
One ancient cedar rears the spot today;
Nearby, the Unknown twenty lie in wake,
Beyond the fevered captain's grave, to sway
The great decision that became their stake.
Emanuel, the Leutze, brushed the feat
Undying art has so immortalized—
The crossing—that New York in worth could meet,
Then lent to us the scene we had not prized.

At the State Park, edged on the Delaware,
Is the requartered frame that we may share.

PHILADELPHIA THEN

The leading city of the colonies,
She reigned with light of heart and grace of mind;
Her regal style, so shaded by green trees,
Refreshed the ancient wreathes that browed mankind.
Still on the wall of Old Christ Church, as then,
King George stares at his own Colonial town,
Remembering that his Tories stayed on when
The rebels made the English law their own.
Here bloomed the buds of Hanoverian seed
With British freedom seeped in Roman lore;
The taverns and the parlors housed the breed
That cloaked the words the Constitution wore.

They wrote the codes by which all laws could later prove
That freedom has the strength to arm the world to move.

THE FLAG

Be it a Rossi or a Betsy Ross,
It matters not who snipped the dawning stars;
Upon the field was made another cross,
The symbol which the lands division bars.
The hands that palm for silver throw the dice
That some may own the cloak of cloth and blood
To cover their blind face, their breast of ice,
And burn the remnant of the ancient rood.
Like beasts, they would their aging parents fell
And coil upon the unfurled flesh and bone;
They leave no stripes, no stellar counts to till
The conquest of a demon draped in stone.

The flag is all the dress a nation wears,
The badge that tests the fabric of who cares.

LIBERTY BELL

Proclaim our liberty throughout the land,
That pitched the wind in Penn's Woods' primal cove,
As one clear note alerted high the band
To rise, sustained in fugues of tonal love.
As phrase caught phrase upon the State House Tower,
The rhythm beat the tune in fifty-one
To swell the sound to ring that dawning hour
Which marked the day when man his freedom won.
As double fifty doubles once again,
The pealing call-up rounds as many states,
A turned baton to orchestrate the reign
Of every man in whom all glory waits.

As imperfection makes true beauty swell,
The crack sound-offs the message of the bell.

ELFRETH'S ALLEY

Today we chant the song, the middle-man,
From North to South in shaded, quiet streets;
The one whose hat is hard works every fan,
And greets the level of the eyes he meets.
But—the proletariat was always here
In Elfreth's Alley's narrow thoroughfare;
We walk the street that cuts the Center where
First William Penn had laid the block, a square.
Stand still to hear the blacksmith's hammered blow,
The swish of river pilots swagging by;
The tailors lacing cloth with velvet show,
The cabinet-makers trudge as trade they ply.

The newer signs, though framing artistry,
Are spinning wheels in fashion's gallery.

PAT LYON AT THE FORGE
Painting by John Neagle

THE POWEL HOUSE

On Third Street, South, two hundred forty-four,
There is a garden with an old pear tree;
It takes us to the nation's first back door,
Where Samuel Powel housed his mayor's key.
The King's Lord High Commissioner took reign
The fashion charm where majesty had come;
Then, Independence honored Powel again,
Who, as first citizen, once more came home.
By him, both George and Martha Washington
Were graced as guests and friends in our old town;
The presence of the President was won
Because he loved our city as his own.

Polling the ward-kings of two-hundred years,
This frank relationship dispels our fears.

THE POWEL HOUSE
Photograph of the Restored Structure

JOHN BARTRAM'S GARDEN

I sometimes walk along the Schuylkill bank,
Where small plantations stand like sentinels,
And stop before the stones of ivied shank
The Swedes had built and left like empty shells.
John Bartram left his father's barn and tree
To search the colonies for every plant;
He gave the world green news of botany;
His letters fed his friends their studied want.
Here in his garden, Eden still grows free,
Unhampered by the serpent's wile and whim;
The doctored science still says less to me
Than structured house had done to hamper him.

Below the window, still is carved in stone
That he adored no man, but God alone.

THE JOHN BARTRAM HOUSE
From an old photograph

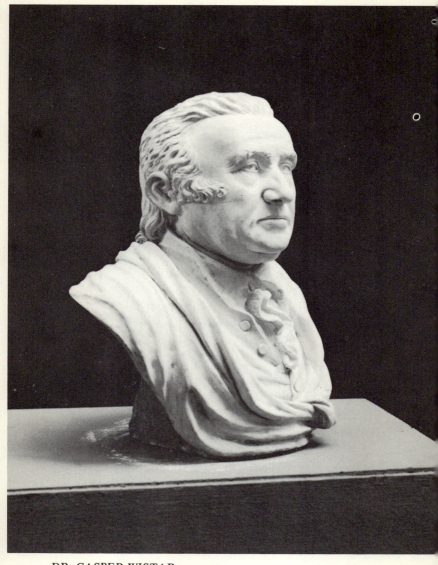

DR. CASPER WISTAR
Terra cotta bust by William Rush

SHIPPEN-WISTAR HOUSE

On torrid days, I seek the Green Tree shade
That marks the Shippen-Wistar House today;
And, in the cool the purple vine has made,
The APA still gathers for its play.
Still, William Shippen walks to Congress rooms
The Continentals hallowed with their plans;
His son the Army wards with comfort grooms,
And greets the southern Lees to share his lands.
My ears are ghosted with those urgent sounds
That Caspar Wistar later must have heard;
The walls defy my voice; a music wounds
The mystic charm of their now sacred word.

The small physician works the great men's hire,
Assuring them against the tyrant's fire.

SOCIETY HILL

The Free Society of Traders set
The chartered course for later companies,
Since William Penn their budding queries met
To build town homes for growing families.
There, not far from Independence Hall,
We walk along as they did long before;
And, having tripped the magic of the Mall,
We toe the streets the projects now restore.
Old Philadelphia exhumes her graves
Where cellar holes were ravished in the Hill;
The Georgian graces have survived the staves,
Reincarnated, musing with us still.

As soon put out the light of ordered star,
As quench the style endemic to our lar.

GLORIA DEI (OLD SWEDES' CHURCH)

The city harbors ethnics at its port,
Besieged like sloughing surfs of hybrid seas;
Abandoned ruins of some former fort
Are ringed by homing rows and industries.
An island isolates its aging heart
That a cathedral in the forest folds,
Where once the Swedes in logs had prayed their part,
But now as Gloria Dei others holds.
The fort of old is near the altar stone;
The Bibles and the relics witness long
The organ gallery, where voices gone
Once joined the cherubs in their Christmas song.

You can, in mind, on Delaware near Christian Street,
Pray at the oldest church, and with Colonials meet.

Swede's Church
Built 1700

OLD SWEDES CHURCH
Nineteenth Century Engraving

MIKVEH ISRAEL

The wandering man finds solace in a wall
That gathers equally the leaf and vine,
And in the embrace finds there resting all
Who slipped the pogroms of forbidden wine.
Here, bricked along the street of lasting spruce,
Our first brave Jews were dignified to lie;
The Mikveh Israel were given truce
To mark their own and none could them defy.
Haym Salomon, real patriarch of theirs,
Was quietly the patriot of ours;
And through these early walls made separate squares,
New ground they unified by seeding flowers.

As their Rebecca Gratz becomes our Esther Klein
The gates are doorways to all cherished friends of mine.

SIMON GRATZ
Plaster bust by L. Drake

CHRIST CHURCH

I dare to praise the Church its Bingo game,
That it upon my foible raise its choir;
As Franklin did with lottery the same
For Christ Church when it needed bell and spire.
There, now, the silver pieces of the queen
Still grace the altar cloth before the arch;
The coral triptych, chandelier are seen
As relics all revere; they Grailed our march.
Our George went there, so Hopkinson and Hewes,
Who rest so well with Morris, Ross, and Rush,
And Wilson; the Declaration's muse
Braced, as they signed with freedom's ink and brush.

Though Magna Carta barons with flags were canonized,
The font was holy made when Penn was there baptized.

CHRIST CHURCH
Painting by William Strickland

OLD ST. JOSEPH'S CHURCH

At first, the anti-Romans hid the keys,
While time-established rites they disapproved;
Like children, bending parents to their knees,
Their infancy with tyranny they moved.
Then, Penn the Father of the Family saw
As the first sage of freedom's holy word;
He gave Saint Joseph place, and bound by law
The right to conscience, that its voice be heard.
In Willing's Alley, still the spirit walks;
The entry hosts the ghosts of former guards.
Hushed, now, are cries of former doves and hawks,
While fading masses whimper from their wards.

As freedom of the spirit allows no Inn to close,
We must still fan the incense with which the altars rose.

OLD ST. JOSEPH'S CHURCH
Joseph Pennell's Engraving of the Gateway

OLD SAINT PETER'S

I somehow know that old Saint Peter beams
Above the Hill, Society of streets;
Although the Roman source relates my dreams,
My pilgrim shoes the Fisherman's here meets.
So white and tall, that needle in the sky
Pricks at the blue that would a cover make;
The New World vision might have neen too high
Had Sam and George disdained their pews to take.
Where, once, their eager spirit plied inside,
The faded colors mark their sketch of lines;
Their peace unravelled strains of the outside
To frame the global commune of high minds.

The power of a Bishop, first to last,
Is here cross-bred by brothers without caste.

THE FIRST STATUE OF LIBERTY
(AT THE LIBRARY COMPANY)

Minerva, goddess of enlightened minds,
Our country's Patroness of Liberty,
With vine leaves on her helmet, wisdom binds
The tie of Congress to the Library.
Where Franklin's Company had first the books
That spelled the spoken words of Congress Hall,
No longer from the Speaker's Desk she looks,
But from her Locust's perch she spies us all.
From her vast view our Citizen is scored
In those first minutes written in his hand;
The Junto had him all their talk record
The first groupthink discussions of the land.

The matrix of our intellect and power,
She timed the ancients to our present hour.

BENJAMIN FRANKLIN

From City Hall, through Logan, to the Park,
The main way bears the name of Benjamin;
Young Franklin brought to us his globe-timed spark
That fused the walls we all could settle in.
The printer's ink for him a fortune made
That he might set his stamp upon his time;
For sixty years of service, worked and played
The first American in worldly rhyme.
In science, public aristocracy,
He drove his duty, made the maxim wide;
His reason fixed our new diplomacy
And pointed to the world our rising tide.

This was the star that marked our governmental fate,
The light that framed the chart of freedom as a state.

ELDER STATESMAN

When this, our kindergarten age, is done,
We shall recall the schoolrooms of the wise,
The pocket-loaf to wealth, youth on the run,
And, finding form-shod Franklins, fit our size.
He served the Continental Congress, one
Of the Committee to make up the five
The Declaration signed; French aid he won,
While ripe with seventy years, each one alive.
At eighty-one, the elder statesman hit
The Constitutional Convention's fate;
He wrote the compromise that sealed the writ,
Then, led three times the council of the state.

The tensile silk of Franklin, mind-strong at eighty-four,
Still holds the hemp of boy-packs thumping on the floor.

BENJAMIN FRANKLIN
Painting by David Martin

POOR RICHARD

Striding campus on a pedestal,
The moment he arrived, now, frozen walks;
His guide, the art of thinking, paced his will
From Ozell to Richard Saunders and his talks.
He pressed the burden of his print so well,
He massed a mound of books without a debt;
To spread the news the paper had to tell,
He bought the Pennsylvania Gazette.
His words, the maxims, ruling colonies,
Translated prosody with lyric knack;
We versify the rules and prophecies
As written in Poor Richard's Almanac.

The logic of a Franklin transcends the printed book;
The magic of his Library is in its binding hook.

FRANKLIN'S HOSPITAL

The mind and spirit serve the flesh and bone
When accident and weakness bend our fate;
For these, our needs, Ben Franklin, not alone,
With Thomas Bond made plans to expiate.
The Hospital they built in fifty-one
Was in America the first we saw;
From the Assembly here the donors won
The match appropriating funds by law.
Today, the site and structure stand the ground
As they held lines two hundred years ago;
Here, many "firsts" in medicine were found,
And many now are scored for all to know.

The Pennsylvania Hospital is Franklin's psalm,
Restoring strength and will with help of coin and balm.

THE GRAVE

In seventeen-ninety, when he died, he left
A simple marking for his resting-place;
The needle scratched in our Green Towne, bereft,
The words of plainness that his actions lace.
So willed by him, a printer he is called,
A government official at the most;
At Fifth and Arch Streets, near a railing, walled
He lies, inscribed, an oracle to host.
You may go there and place a copper coin,
A votive to Poor Richard's memory;
Thus, I, from Trevi ancestors, will join
With you to share the city's history.

Each moment of our time is gold we spend,
That we may write inscriptions of our end.

FIRE INSURANCE COMPANY

With us, insurance is a prize we earned,
That Franklin offered first in fifty-two;
Contributionship replaced what fire burned,
So constitutionals might start anew.
Just as, in the fall, the compost of the soil
Secures the nitrates for the seeds of spring,
That, with the daily turn of human toil,
The promised hour of the flowers bring;
So did the company of Hand-in-Hand
Protect by policy a processed pile
That could replace the charred-out home and land,
And build anew with planted deed on file.

On Fourth Street Franklin led the early registry,
And housed America its oldest company.

THE UNIVERSITY

The impetus his first Proposals whet
To teach the youth in Pennsylvania,
With Franklin's flair, became the luring net
To fund the walls of academia.
First president of the trustees, he veered
The sporing school to more diversity;
In ninety-one, as he the board-mates steered,
He charted Penn, our University.
Like a new grape some vintner's secret brew
In due time to ferment the rarest wine,
The rod of learning into acres grew
With vineyards, groves whose leafings twine with mine.

From Franklin Field to where the ivied towers sway,
Youth circles still to hallow the enlightened way.

AMERICAN PHILOSOPHICAL SOCIETY

On Independence Square a quiet wall
Recalls the Virtuosi of like kind;
The red-brick face of Philosophical Hall
Refracts nine eyes for culture cats gone blind.
Promoting Useful Knowledge was the aim
That Franklin gave the group in forty-three;
With letters piling pyramids of fame,
They reamed their documents for history.
Across Fifth Street the Library now stands,
Twin pillars of Ben Franklin's Company;
His manuscripts and books fulfill demands,
Gemmed artifacts that scholars here mine free.

Refreshing for us all, the open Square we find,
The only privacy housed there to greet the mind.

BROADCASTING HIS NAME

You hear of Franklin all around the town,
In row house courts, in streets and boulevards;
For science, research centers make him known,
And in his name the Towers grace the yards.
Near us, a meadow, wild with ripened wheat,
Was stripped by hungry crows that raped its grains;
Then came in time, a veteran hand to beat
The sound transmitting thunder from the rains.
The single-noted title found its score,
A podium of music for old Ben;
Where his charged kite the heaven's lightning tore
Is now the wave-length lettered FLN.

Philadelphia has the classic to broadcast his name,
The Station Houston, Smith, and Green have
      brought to fame.

PHILADELPHIA, THE LIVING CITY

The Living City, like a phoenix grows
Around the Girard Plaza heliport;
The dome, with shoulders feathering no repose,
Soars over buildings, nests of work and sport.
Its out-stretched wings arm w rds of human care;
Its mind stays beamed to lamps of learning light;
The finest music waves the channeled air,
Where we may knob the patterns day and night.
Regeneration is its rhythmic keel
That balances the house, the bank, and store;
From Penn's Landing to this Eastern Square you feel
The flight that circles to the past with more.

From global ash, our Port and corporate will now rise,
A flame-tensed monument to private enterprise.

CONVENTION CITY

Prime model of conventions, as was here
The Continental, Constitutional,
The central place, convenient without peer,
The hospitality, traditional.
The Civic Center shows the peoples' stall,
Banked on the Schuylkill, river to the west,
With meeting rooms, Museum, and a Hall
For sports and entertainments ranking best.
A Panorama moves to flick our town,
Framed by exhibits flown from everywhere;
A concert hummed by all, a craft unknown—
It matters not; all effort gathers there.

The beat that pulses at the city's heart
Vibrates the measures of its life and art.

THE CITY'S SQUARES

She is the sum of circles bound in squares
Where God once hubbed his largest wagon wheel;
Her veil of green for little walks she wears
Where tiny plots are ringed by glass and steel.
Once Thomas Holme designed the Country Towne
And lined the streets and quadrants with new trees;
Penn's Square her mansion centered as her own;
Northwest, the Logan tulips catch the breeze.
In Rittenhouse, art lines flick in the sun;
Northeast, the waters cool old Franklin Square;
Southeast, the Georgian brick fronts Washington
To house her mother's sons still settled there.

Two miles in length and one in breadth were crossed
To cap her brow from which the crown she tossed.

FOURTH OF JULY IN CENTER SQUARE
Painting by John Lewis Krimmel

THE PRESIDENTIAL MANSIONS

Three Presidential Mansions stood in grace
Like goddesses that charmed our myths to fact;
The beauty of all time is on their face;
Their youth endures the ravages of act.
The first, the Robert Morris House, is drawn
At the Atwater Kent, in model built;
At Ninth and Chestnut, reject stands forlorn,
The unused house that Adams shied with guilt.
When yellow fever raged in seventy-three,
Our ruling bloods rushed out to Germantown;
At Isaac Franks our Washingtons made free
The Deshler-Morris House to make their own.

As reigning diadems are crowned by hours,
The dowager, the "First White House" is ours.

BI-WITNESSES

In slavery birthed, two ministers of God
Raised temples to the star-shine of the mind,
That to the darkness left the whip and rod,
Transcending sale and crush of humankind.
The Free African Society they formed
In eighty-seven paved their highway march
To battle low-keyed in each church reformed
From blacksmith's ring or from the stiffest starch.
For Saint Thomas or the simple Methodist,
The Priests were African Episcopals;
On Parrish Street there is no twilight mist
To shade the dawning of the principals.

They point to Philadelphia's high noon,
For everyone the bright side of the moon.

PHILADELPHIA'S NAVAL ACADEMY

Annapolis had its young mother here
At twenty-fourth where Grays Ferry is crossed;
The marbled temple wears a classic gear,
South Philadelphia we never lost.
Built in the thirties for our midshipmen,
The first Naval Academy grew fast;
Transferred in eighty-five, her home, as then,
As the State's Naval Home is cast.
The genesis, that schooled our Navy men
And was asylum to their age and pain,
Is still the teacher now as she was then;
Her voices float above the winds again.

There is a magic to the South, you feel,
That kites the winning captains at its keel.

BANK OF THE UNITED STATES

The keeper of the coin, another first,
Banked with the Carpenters in ninety-one;
Transplant of England, checking growing thirst,
Its treasure logged the books of Hamilton.
The cuttings grew to force the load to move
To its platform on Chestnut Street and Third;
But its new strength piled through to leaves above,
Until Girard milled it, the loss to gird.
As Information Center now it stands
In the Historical Park for you to see;
The Nation's oldest bank, the building hands
The rolls to guide your pathways; chips are free.

While Temples reach to move the eye to lift the soul,
The pillars roof the gold to shod our feet for shoal.

MUSEUMS

Our city glories in its specialty
From sculptures of Rodin to ethnic rooms:
The Perelman Toys, The University,
The Muetter Medicine, The Civic Center booms;
The Army, Naval, and the Maritime,
Marine, and U.S.S. Olympia,
All verse with homes and sites to make the rhyme
Compose one EAC—Philadelphia.
The dancing mummers, costumed artifacts,
All bound in common consciousness of kind,
Are fractured frames of the genetic pacts
The pioneers have to us left behind.

What archeology and science show in proof
Support the walls for human art to make the roof.

THE ART MUSEUM

The Renaissance gave us the classic world,
Renewing us with roots from buried parts;
The Art Museum needs no flag unfurled
To crest it as the Palace of the arts.
Five hundred thousand master works and more—
Cezanne, Degas, Picasso, and Duchamp,
With Renoir, and French rooms help make the store
From Gothic chapel to the Bourbon stamp.
The fashion wings, the ancient bric-a-brac
Pre-history and ours have pressed in time;
Man's measured artifacts from crown to sack
Are side by side like opposites in rhyme.

This pile contains the relics of our years;
All time sustains the now to stem our fears.

THE ART ALLIANCE

The Art Alliance knits upon the square
A tapestry of creativity.
All forms and patterns radiate the air
That blows the scarf of stress or levity.
Where once the Wetherills held court with grace,
And windows faced the grass of Rittenhouse
To hold the view for thousands in the place,
Now spring the artists with the silvered douse.
The gush of waters nourishes each wound
The demon festers for creative act
In print, in stone, on canvas, stage with sound,
For whom the patrons turn the dream to fact.

All Philadelphia Arts are centered here,
One cultural arena with no peer.

PENNSYLVANIA ACADEMY OF THE FINE ARTS

One block away, by North of City Hall,
You leave the bottom fog of office rain;
While winds storm mayors in their rise or fall,
Walk past the curb to find the sun again.
The Academy of the Fine Arts waits there,
The first our nation mothered in her pride,
The marriage act of her old love affair
With the hard dreamer of the windmill's ride.
In Independence Hall in eighteen five
These chambers walled the light of weathered hands;
From their caresses masters came alive,
The Peale's the West's, the teachers of new lands.

A museum is a beauty-making tool
To model for the program of its school.

THE ACADEMY OF MUSIC

On Broad and Locust Streets the Palace stands
The Philadelphia Orchestra calls home;
The Whole World's Symphony the master's hands
Direct to lift the music to the dome.
It soars on air-waves with its global sound
In concerts, shaking stars from heaven's lair;
And, resonating caves of hidden ground,
Its tunes seduce the dragon and the bear.
The Grand Old Lady in her plain old cape
Reveals her gold and marble dress to see;
Though we, in seventy-six, her birthday shape,
She crowned her hundred years in seventy-three.

This goddess with no distant voice surpassed,
Her moving arts give vision to her cast.

THE ACADEMY OF NATURAL SCIENCES

At Nineteenth and the Parkway, spend an hour,
Or more, to watch the Whole Earth come alive;
Pause; say "hello" to one dinosaur;
Then wander, brushing by a cave or hive.
Our country's first museum of its kind,
It houses quadrupeds in nature's frame;
The dioramas move you in your mind
To distant haunts, seducing you by name.
You suddenly find strange communion here
With every creature breathing in the air;
You sense the unison of atmosphere,
The cosmic dust of life-spans that you share.

This is the world, the glove without an end;
The circle makes us each another's friend.

FAIRMOUNT PARK

Preened glens and beauty's regimen of fields,
You rabbit-patch the cabbage yards beyond;
Four thousand acres, growing Fairmount yields
The gentlest span that banks the global pond.
The circle and the square of life are here,
Where each green niche protects a work of art,
Reflected by the loving atmosphere
Embracing this live bower of the heart.
The people empty here to do their will.
To bicycle, to jog, to park, or sail,
Play cricket, rugby, other games, until
With ride or swim they make our peace prevail

The Arts, the Zoo, the Playhouse, and the Dell
Among the trees have cast the human spell.

FAIRMOUNT WATERWORKS
Painting by Thomas Birch

MONUMENTAL

Model, patronizing all the arts,
Sister city of the Arno queen,
We touch and climb, then hide within our hearts
The monuments, the ideals that have been.
Wolff's Lion fighter, Rush's Schuylkill Freed
Are tempered by Abe Lincoln Rogers caught,
Like Sailor's Navigator, Kemey's breed,
And Bailly's Washington the City bought.
The sport, Diana and the Duck Girl chose,
Gaul's Eagle and Tedyuscung spark;
As Schwarzman's Art reflects the Premiere Pose
That dawned the golden deed of Joan of Arc.

Strangling Prometheus through Age of Bronze moves on,
While the Great Mother waters still the unknown Swann.

THE HISTORICAL SOCIETY OF PENNSYLVANIA

No monument nor field sights history
To lens the past with instant news today
Like our Historical Society
Of Pennsylvania, with all to say.
The plan of Philadelphia, of Holme's,
In eighty-one lined for our Country Towne,
Near Wilson's drafted Constitution roams
To square the spaced collections so renown.
The manuscripts, the papers, and the books
Vie with the portraits, prints, and furniture;
First wampum, photograph, and New Deal works
Are programmed in our current literature.

The genealogy, the draft, the stored event,
Await the scholar here, who on research is bent.

THE SPECTRUM

Sports Town, U.S.A., our other name,
Has birthed a major team in every league;
Two million townsmen cheered the Flyers' fame
To win the Stanley Cup without intrigue.
The outdoor games in Veteran's Stadium
Are verve and spirit of our spatial home;
In history we match the Colosseum
With our new Spectrum, arena with a dome.
Three stadiums within three miles of town
Have triple-crowned the running of our plays;
Competing to make victory our own
Makes blossoms of our newly budding days.

You come here both the class and team to find
The all we need to firm the muscle and the mind.

THE COUNTRY MANSIONS

The city's lineage is sealed in homes
That wax their signature on Park and tar;
The Hill where Platt the Oval Parlor roams
Had lemons when the Morris pursed the war.
The Woodford Mansion Coleman held so dear,
Whose altar stone the Colonies had graced,
Walls still Naomi Wood in "household gear,"
The model rooms to which our own are traced.
To Belmont, where young Peters sought the peace,
Our playgoers rush now to chat and dine;
But, Sweetbrier to Breck gives new release
For "Recollections" of old talk and wine.

From Strawberry to Pleasant, paths have made us warm;
The first society has roofed us with its charm.

MT. PLEASANT
Watercolor by D. J. Kennedy

THE HISTORIC COUNTRY HOUSES

The Whitemarsh Valley pets in its embrace
The pacing homes of Shackamaxon's past;
The Highlands and Hope Lodge still lift their face,
And rub their fingers on your fresh-formed cast.
Not far beyond, you come to Sandy Run
The seventy-twenty Emlens opened wide,
Where, marching through the forges, Washington
Lay down to rest from the assaults outside.
With powder dried, the social heads curled back
To grace the mansions ringing Philadelphia;
Set like a diamond on a classic stack,
The Biddles glove the flash of Andalusia.

The historic country houses are jewels matched in prime
Their lustre grows with wearing, a patina touched by time.

STENTON
From a Wood engraving

PHILADELPHIA, TO THE SOUTH

They hanged the Christ to balance the condemned
Beyond the reason where the law could go;
And no one knew the cause why two were hemmed
Like Columbus, Addonizio.
Like bees in chorus, their antennae ringed,
They swarmed and buzzed to hide in fragile hives;
The yeomen hurled the rocks; the dons were winged,
And aping militants plunged in their knives.
Then, in this city where old brothers loved
And cradled once the genesis of law,
The Roman once again by reason proved
That right ignores the executor's flaw.

Dissenters and their parasites contract
To fault the ethnic's crucifying fact.

GERMANTOWN

You must take time to see old Germantown.
The first thirteen Pastorius took there
In eighty-three, northwest, to farm their own
Joined industry, academy to share.
The Mennonites built strong their meeting house
To guard the market-shed, the stocks, and jail.
Pulp stocked the paper mill of Riitenhouse;
Bricks graced the Concord School, the quarried vale.
At Grumblethorpe we dream of summer moods,
Of redcoats sounding horn for fox and hound;
We touch the stones and trees of Wister's Woods,
Reflect the peace, the upper Burying Ground.

As freely as the first who paced the market square,
The shaded streets converge the many people there.

THE PHILADELPHIA SOUND

"Oh, dem golden slippers," have been spiked
To heel the tarantella's faster beat;
The sound of Philadelphia has been hiked
To scale the steps, a stage above the street.
A hurdy-gurdy, groan of long ago,
Still grinds below the shuffled Mummer's song;
The feathers bend like tree-boughs to the flow
Of household gods the dancers bring along.
The rhythms by Acadians have been toned
To grace the banjos with soft mandolins;
The heavy boot-steps are now tapped and honed
To square quick measures when the march begins.

In the breeze on key the Druid waves his hoary hair,
Teased by the Roman spider spinning in the air.